THE ANCIENT GREEKS

JOHN MALAM

WAYLAND

HISTORY STARTS HERE!
The Ancient Greeks
OTHER TITLES IN THE SERIES
The Ancient Egyptians • The Ancient Romans
The Aztecs • The Tudors • The Victorians

Produced for Wayland Publishers Limited by
Roger Coote Publishing
Gissing's Farm
Fressingfield
Suffolk IP21 5SH
England

Designer: Victoria Webb
Editor: Alex Edmonds
Illustrations: Michael Posen
Cover artwork: Kasia Posen

First published in 1999 by Wayland Publishers Limited
61 Western Road, Hove, East Sussex BN3 1JD

British Library Cataloguing in Publication Data
Malam, John
  The ancient Greeks. – (History starts here)
  1.Greece – History – To 146 BC. – Juvenile literature
  2.Greece – Civilization – To 146 BC. – Juvenile literature
  I.Title
  938

ISBN 0 7502 2367 7

Printed and bound in Italy
by G. Canale & C.S.p.A., Turin

Front cover picture: A Greek vase from the fifth century BC, showing
women washing clothes.
Title page picture: A vase showing women making offerings to the gods.

Picture acknowledgements:
AKG London Ltd: 6, 10, 14 (Erich Lessing), 15 (Alfons Rath), 22 (John Hios),
27 (Erich Lessing); Ancient Art and Architecture Collection 18 (R Sheridan),
23 (R Sheridan), 29 (M&J Lynch); British Museum 1, 17; CM Dixon: 7, 8, 13, 19, 21, 24,
25, 26, 28; ET Archive: front cover; Tony Stone Images: 4 (George Grigoriou),
9 (Mervyn Rees), 10–11 (George Grigoriou), 20 (Robert Everts).

All Wayland books encourage children to
read and help them improve their literacy.

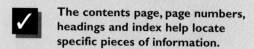 The contents page, page numbers,
headings and index help locate
specific pieces of information.

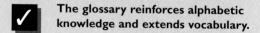 The glossary reinforces alphabetic
knowledge and extends vocabulary.

The further information section
suggests other books dealing with
the same subject.

find Wayland on the Internet at http://www.wayland.co.uk

CONTENTS

WHO WERE THE GREEKS?

Greece is a country in the south of Europe. It is warm and sunny and is almost completely surrounded by sea. There are many rugged mountains. They run across the land in long lines, called ranges.

Because much of Greece is covered in mountains, the Greeks have always lived by the sea, where the land is flatter and easier to farm.

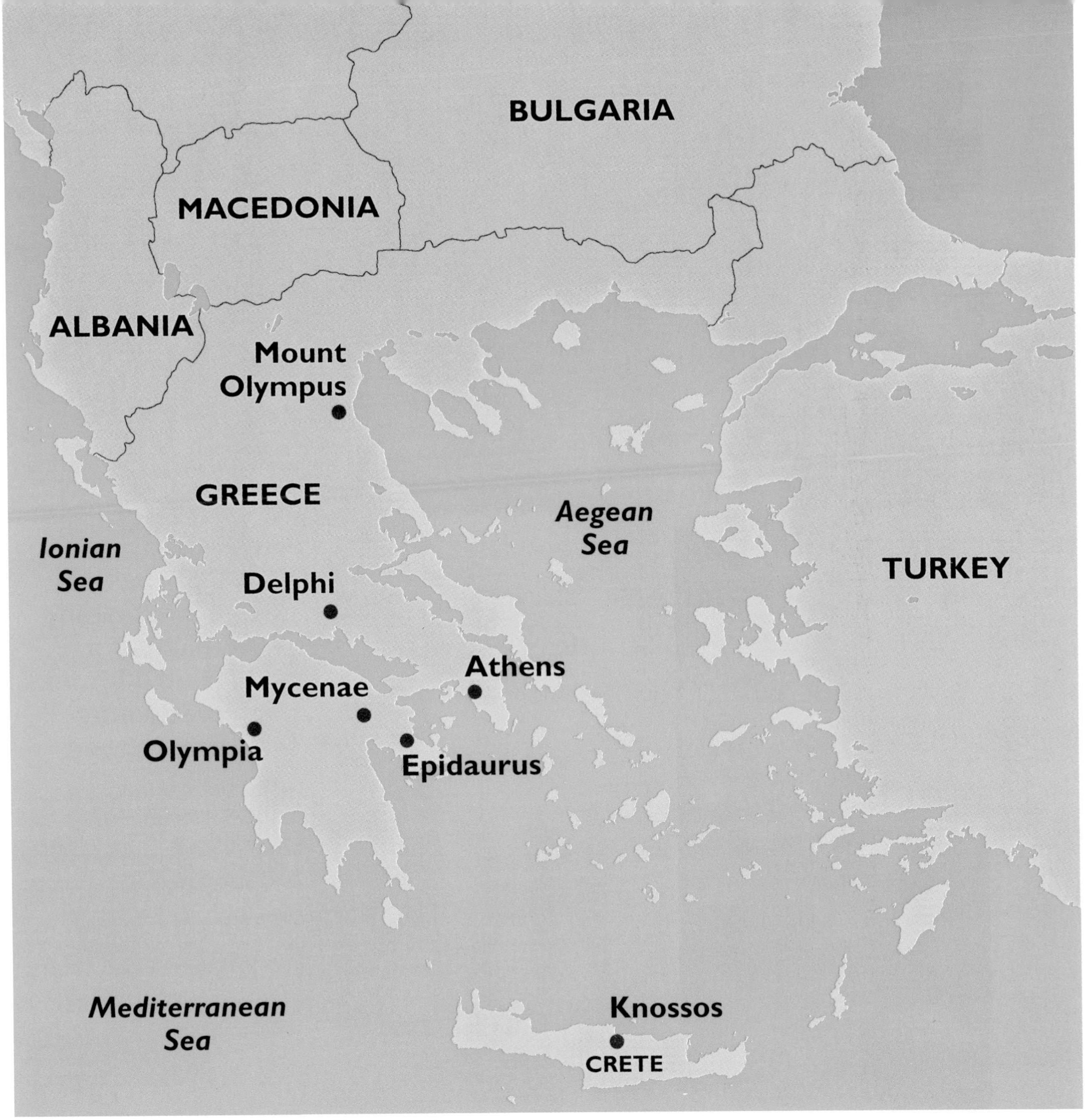
BULGARIA
MACEDONIA
ALBANIA
Mount Olympus
GREECE
Aegean Sea
Ionian Sea
TURKEY
Delphi
Athens
Mycenae
Olympia
Epidaurus
Mediterranean Sea
Knossos
CRETE

This map shows how the mainland part of Greece is joined to other countries in Europe. About 2,000 islands belong to Greece. Less than 200 of them have people living on them.

It was here, more than 2,000 years ago, that the ancient Greeks lived. They created one of the world's first important civilizations. Some of the things we have today, such as the alphabet, the theatre and the Olympic Games were started all those years ago by the ancient Greeks.

THE BEGINNING OF GREECE

The Minoans and the Mycenaeans were the first two important groups of people in Greece.

The Minoans lived on Crete and other islands nearby. They built palaces with many rooms. They farmed the land and fished and hunted. They also knew how to write. The Minoans had their own language, which was not Greek.

This Minoan picture shows people leaping over the back of a charging bull. This was a game that young Minoan men played.

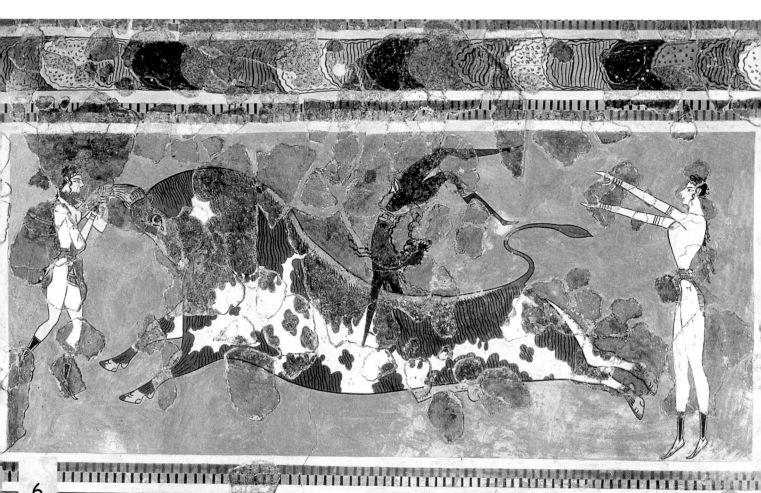

The city of Mycenae was built on top of a hill. Its strong walls protected the town from attackers.

The Mycenaeans lived on the mainland. They lived in towns around the city of Mycenae and were ruled over by kings. The Mycenaeans spoke a type of Greek. They are said to be the first Greeks.

The Minoans and the Mycenaeans lived about 4,000 years ago and they traded with each other. The idea of writing spread from the Minoans to the Mycenaeans. Then, about 3,000 years ago, both civilizations came to an end.

ATHENS - CITY OF MARBLE

The Greeks who lived after the Mycenaeans built many towns and cities. One city, called Athens, became more powerful than all the rest.

Athens was at its most powerful 2,500 years ago. It was a busy city. As many as 200,000 people lived there and in the countryside around. Athens owned valuable silver mines, and, like other Greek cities, had its own army. It had a fleet of warships, too.

Pericles was a great leader in Athens. He ordered the Parthenon to be built.

On top of a high hill stood a group of beautiful temples. They were built from marble, which is a hard white stone. The grandest temple of all was the Parthenon.

The Parthenon was once painted in bright colours, but the paint has worn away. It was built to honour the goddess Athena.

HOW A CITY WAS RUN

The ancient Greeks invented a form of government called 'democracy'. This means 'power by the people'. It was a fair system because the citizens of Greece could decide how they wanted their city to be run.

An unpopular man could be sent away from the city if the citizens of Athens voted for him to go. They voted on pieces of broken pottery, called *Ostraka*.

In Athens, citizens held their meetings in the open air on the Pnyx hill. Its name meant 'packing place'.

Greek citizens chose their own leaders, made laws, and decided whether to go to war or not. Citizens were men born in the city, whose parents had been born there, too. It did not matter if they were rich or poor.

GREEK CITIZENS

Only some people were allowed to be citizens of the city where they lived. Women, slaves and outsiders from other Greek cities or foreign lands, could not be citizens.

LIFE IN ANCIENT GREECE

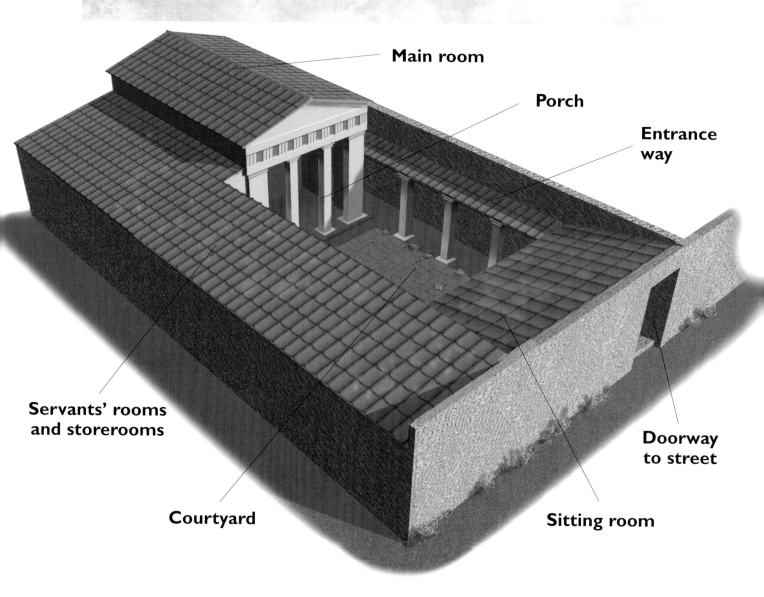

Main room

Porch

Entrance way

Servants' rooms and storerooms

Doorway to street

Courtyard

Sitting room

This is how a Greek house might have looked. Everyday life centred around the courtyard. This was where children played, where food was cooked, and where visitors were met.

People lived in houses built from bricks of clay. Walls were painted white to keep the heat of the Sun out. Houses had several rooms, placed around a courtyard. There were separate rooms for women, men, guests and slaves. The main room was for feasting and entertaining guests.

A woman was expected to stay at home and look after the household. She cooked, cleaned and cared for the children. She made the family's clothes. If the family had slaves, she gave them orders.

Men were free to come and go from the house as they wished. They went to work, bought food in the market square and visited temples and festivals.

This woman is spinning wool to make cloth.

CHILDREN AND SCHOOL

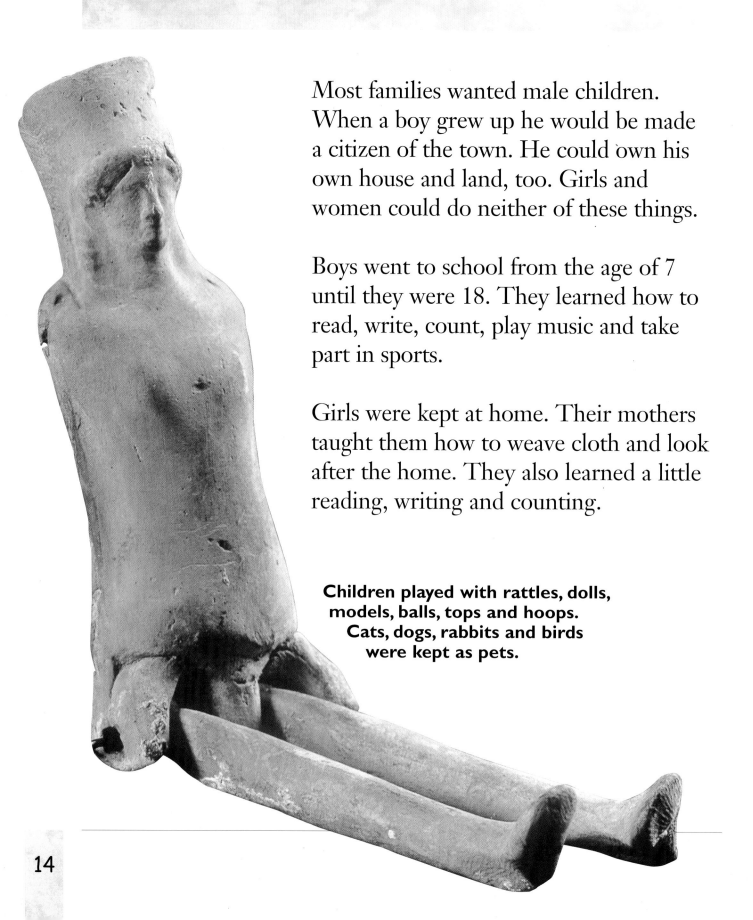

Most families wanted male children. When a boy grew up he would be made a citizen of the town. He could own his own house and land, too. Girls and women could do neither of these things.

Boys went to school from the age of 7 until they were 18. They learned how to read, write, count, play music and take part in sports.

Girls were kept at home. Their mothers taught them how to weave cloth and look after the home. They also learned a little reading, writing and counting.

Children played with rattles, dolls, models, balls, tops and hoops. Cats, dogs, rabbits and birds were kept as pets.

There were 24 letters in the Greek alphabet. The word 'alphabet' comes from the names of the first two Greek letters, *alpha* and *beta*.

GREEK CLOTHES

Warm clothes were woven from sheeps' wool. The flax plant was used to make linen, which was thinner and lighter than wool.

A man dressed for travelling. He wears a short cloak, a hat to keep the sun off his head, and leather walking boots with laces.

DYES

Clothes were usually left a natural creamy-white colour. Sometimes dyes were used. Yellow dye was made from part of the crocus flower. Red came from the leaves of the madder plant. Purple came from the crushed shells of sea snails.

Because a lot of cloth was used in Greek clothes, they hung in neat, loose folds from the shoulders and waist.

Most Greek clothes were made from rectangular-shaped material. The material was draped around the body and pins, brooches and belts fastened it in place. Men, women and children wore similar styles of clothing.

Most people had short hair. If a woman had long hair, she might tie it up with ribbons.

FOOD AND DRINK

Bread, biscuits and porridge were the main foods eaten by everyone. They were all made from barley, which grew in Greece.

This painting on a vase shows olives being knocked from a tree with sticks. Oil was squeezed from olives, which grew well in Greece. It was used in cooking, and in lamps where it was burned to give light.

Farmers grew vegetables in their fields and sold them in the town's market square. They grew beans, peas, lentils, cabbages, cucumbers, lettuces, leeks, onions and garlic. They gathered walnuts, chestnuts and hazelnuts. Fruit crops were apples, pears, olives, grapes, dates and figs.

The Greeks ate meat from sheep, pigs, cattle and birds, as well as fish.

Most feasts were for men only. They ate and drank in the main room of the house, while lying on couches.

GODS AND GODDESSES

The ancient Greeks had many gods. Because people wanted the gods to protect and help them, they gave them presents. Some gave gifts of food and wine. The greatest gift was an animal, such as a sheep or a goat. It was killed by a priest, and prayers were spoken.

People thought their wishes would be granted if the gifts pleased the gods. Farmers prayed for good harvests. Travellers prayed for safe journeys and the sick prayed for good health.

The Greeks built great Temples to please their gods. People from all over Greece went to this temple at Delphi to pray to Apollo, the god of healing.

20

This is Poseidon, the god of the sea. Statues often show him holding a three-pronged fish spear, called a trident.

Poseidon was a brother of Zeus, the king of the gods. Zeus was the god of weather. Statues often show him throwing a thunder bolt.

FESTIVALS AND GAMES

At a festival, people relaxed and enjoyed themselves. It was time to celebrate and give thanks to the gods. Colourful processions were held.

Sports festivals were always popular. The greatest of all was the Olympic Games. This took place once every four years at Olympia. The festival lasted five days.

It was at the racetrack in Olympia that most of the events took place. The pentathlon was a mix of five different athletic events that each competitor had to enter.

Athletes in ancient Greece did not wear clothes. The paintings on this vase show athletes being presented with prizes at the games.

Men from all parts of Greece, and from overseas too, went to Olympia to take part in the games. Women were not allowed to go there. A winning athlete was given a crown of olive branches. He brought honour to his city by winning at the games.

STORIES AND THEATRE

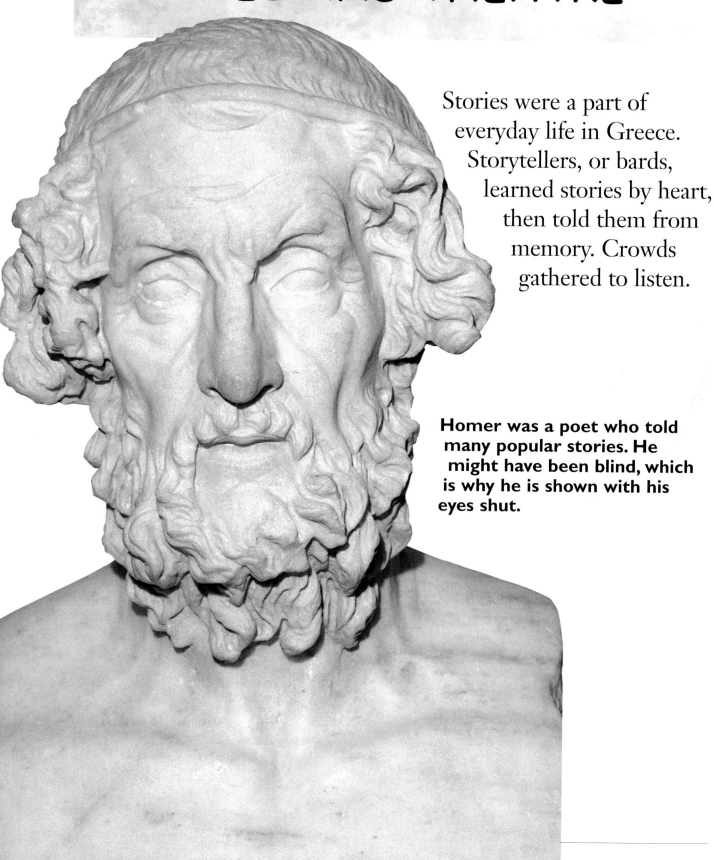

Stories were a part of everyday life in Greece. Storytellers, or bards, learned stories by heart, then told them from memory. Crowds gathered to listen.

Homer was a poet who told many popular stories. He might have been blind, which is why he is shown with his eyes shut.

People liked to go to the theatre. Actors wore masks and costumes, and put on lots of different plays. All the actors were men. Some plays were funny and some were serious. They were set in the past and told stories about gods and heroes.

You can see from this theatre at Epidaurus how the audience sat in the open air on stone seats. Plays were performed in the daytime.

THE GREEKS AT WAR

The ancient Greeks fought many battles. Greek cities argued and fought wars with each other as well as with other countries.

The Greeks went to war with the Persians, who wanted to invade Athens. The Athenians were led by a great commander, Themistocles. At Salamis they fought a great sea battle. The Persians were beaten and they lost 400 ships.

Greek warships had battering rams. They smashed into enemy ships and made big holes in their wooden sides to sink them.

Greek soldiers fought with swords and long spears. They wore armour to protect their bodies.

THE END OF THE GREEKS

The most famous Greek soldier was Alexander. Under his leadership, the Greeks controlled land from Greece to India. After Alexander the Great died, his empire was split up into smaller parts. Greece became less powerful.

Many years later, the Romans came from Italy, to the west of Greece. They built a powerful empire of their own. Greece became part of it.

Alexander was a hero. Because he was such a great leader, he became known as Alexander the Great.

This is a temple which the Romans built in France. It was copied from the style of temples the Greeks built.

The ancient Greeks have taught us many things. Their influence can still be seen today in our art, our sport and the way our countries are governed.

THE ROMANS
The Romans liked the Greeks and the way they lived. They admired the style of their buildings, which they copied, and they based their alphabet on the Greek alphabet. They also enjoyed Greek plays and poetry.

IMPORTANT DATES

All the dates in this list are 'BC' dates. This stands for 'Before Christ'. BC dates are counted back from the year 0, which is the year we say Jesus Christ was born. Some dates have the letter 'c.' in front of them. This stands for 'circa', which means 'about'. These dates are guesses, because no one knows what the real date is.

2000 BC The very first Greek-speaking people arrived in mainland Greece.

c.2000 BC The Minoans built palaces on Crete.

c.1900 BC The Mycenaeans built towns on mainland Greece.

1600 BC Mycenae flourishes.

c.1400 BC The first Greek writing was made. The town of Mycenae was at its greatest.

c.1200 BC The traditional date of the Trojan War.

c.1100 BC The Minoan and Mycenaean civilizations came to an end.

800–500 BC The Archaic Period. The time when ancient Greece began to expand and grow rich.

c.800 BC The Greeks make their own language.

c.800 BC Homer, the greatest Greek poet, lived.

776 BC The first Olympic Games were held.

753 BC Rome was founded.

753 BC Greek poetry became very famous.

500–336 BC The Classical Age. The period when Athens went to war with the Persians and Pericles was leader of Athens.

534 BC The first Greek tragedy was performed.

c.500 BC Democracy was introduced in Athens.

490 BC The Greeks beat the Persians in a battle on land.

480 BC The Greeks beat the Persians in a battle at sea.

479–431 BC The Golden Age. The period when Athens became a wealthy and popular city.

447–438 BC The Parthenon was built in Athens.

431–404 BC Athens lost a war with Sparta, another city in Greece.

430 BC Plague in Athens.

359–336 BC The reign of King Philip II.

338 BC King Philip II conquered and became the ruler of Greece.

336 BC King Philip II died. His son, Alexander, took over from him.

327 BC Alexander's army conquered the Persian army.

323 BC Alexander died, and his empire broke up.

146 BC Greece became part of the Roman Empire.

GLOSSARY

Bard Another name for a storyteller.
Citizen A Greek who was born a free man, and who had a say in how he wanted his town to be run.
Democracy A type of government in which ordinary people have a say in how they want things to be done.
Marble A hard white stone.
Minoans A group of people who lived on Crete and other islands nearby.
Mount Olympus A mountain in the north of Greece where the gods lived.
Mycenaeans A group of people who lived mostly on the mainland of Greece.

Olympians The name given to the family of twelve major gods and goddesses.
Olympic Games The most important festival of sport.
Persians People who lived in Persia, now called Iran.
Poseidon The god of the sea.
Servant Someone who works for another person.
Slave Someone who is owned by another person.
Zeus The king of the gods. He was the god of the weather.

FURTHER INFORMATION

BOOKS TO READ
I Was There: Ancient Greece by John D. Clare (The Bodley Head, 1993)
See Through History: Ancient Greece by Rowena Loverance and Tim Wood (Hamlyn, 1992)

Ancient Greeks at a Glance by John Malam (Macdonald Young Books, 1998)
Ancient Greece: Gods and Goddesses by John Malam (Wayland, 1999)

The Greeks by Susan Peach and Anne Millard (Usborne, 1990)
Ancient Greece by Anne Pearson (Dorling Kindersley Eyewitness Guides, 1992)

INDEX